THE
GREAT GOD
PAN

BOOKS BY AMY HERZOG
PUBLISHED BY TCG

4000 Miles and *After the Revolution*

The Great God Pan

Belleville (forthcoming)

THE
GREAT GOD
PAN

Amy Herzog

THEATRE COMMUNICATIONS GROUP
NEW YORK
2014

The Great God Pan is published by Theatre Communications Group, Inc., 520 8th Avenue, 24th Floor, New York, NY 10018-4156

The verse cited on pages 45–46 and 68 are from "A Musical Instrument," Elizabeth Barrett Browning, circa 1860.

The publication of *The Great God Pan*, by Amy Herzog, through TCG's Book Program, is made possible in part by the New York State Council on the Arts with the support of Governor Andrew Cuomo and the New York State Legislature.

Special thanks to Paula Marie Black for her generous support of this publication.

TCG books are exclusively distributed to the book trade by Consortium Book Sales and Distribution.

LIBRARY OF CONGRESS CATALOGING-IN-PUBLICATION DATA
Herzog, Amy.
The Great God Pan / Amy Herzog.
pages cm
ISBN 978-1-55936-444-7 (pbk.)
ISBN 978-1-55936-753-0 (ebook)
I. Title.
PS3608.E79G74   2014
812'.6—dc23   2013045648

Book design and composition by Lisa Govan
Cover design by Carol Devine Carson

First Edition, February 2014

THE
GREAT GOD
PAN

PRODUCTION HISTORY

The Great God Pan was commissioned by Steppenwolf Theatre
Company and was written with the support of The Orchard
Project/The Exchange. The play received its world premiere
at Playwrights Horizons (Tim Sanford, Artistic Director;
Leslie Marcus, Managing Director) in New York City, on
December 18, 2012. It was directed by Carolyn Cantor; the
set design was by Mark Wendland, the costume design was
by Kaye Voyce, the lighting design was by Japhy Weideman
and the sound design was by Darron L West. The production
stage manager was Cole P. Bonenberger. The cast was:

JAMIE	Jeremy Strong
FRANK	Keith Nobbs
PAIGE	Sarah Goldberg
CATHY	Becky Ann Baker
DOUG	Peter Friedman
JOELLE	Erin Wilhelmi
POLLY	Joyce Van Patten

Scene One

*Two men in their early thirties having coffee. Jamie is a good-looking
and fairly clean-cut Brooklynite; Frank is a multiple-pierced, some-
what effeminate, wounded soul. They make an unlikely duo.*

*A short pause where they wonder who will take responsibility
for the conversation.*

FRANK: . . . and have you seen Polly?

JAMIE: I visited her in the home—was it last summer? It might
have been two years ago now.

FRANK: The home?

JAMIE: She's in a nursing home.

FRANK: Is she that old?

JAMIE: She's gotta be in her eighties.

FRANK: *Really?*

JAMIE: Well she was in her fifties when we were little.

FRANK: Was she?

JAMIE *(Now unsure)*: I think so. Yeah.

FRANK: I think of her as like thirty-five.

JAMIE: Huh. No, she's older than our parents.

FRANK: Is she still . . . with it? Or—

JAMIE: Uhh . . . *(He makes a "comme ci, comme ça" gesture)* She knew who I was, but. It was definitely really sad.

FRANK: She was such a good babysitter.

JAMIE: The best.

FRANK: Do you remember the signs of spring?

JAMIE: The—?

FRANK: She would point out all the signs of spring, each one, as it . . . like the snowdrops, and then the crocuses, and the buds on the—she called it the signs of spring, you don't remember?

JAMIE: I have a terrible memory.

FRANK: I still think about that, every year.

JAMIE: If I visit her—*when* I visit her again, I'll bring that up, she'll love that. She'll be happy that we saw each other.

FRANK: It's great that you've stayed in touch with her.

JAMIE: Well my parents stayed in touch with her better, especially before she went to the home. You guys moved such a long time ago.

FRANK: I think about that a lot, how my life would have been different if my dad hadn't gotten that job. If I had stayed in Highland Park, kept going to Polly's, gone to school with you.

JAMIE: Who knows.

FRANK: But you were always her favorite.

JAMIE: Uh . . .

FRANK: No you were. Smart, and well-behaved.

JAMIE: Well. I don't know.

And you're—in Ithaca now?

FRANK: Yup. Yeah. With my boyfriend.

JAMIE: Uh-huh. What do you do?

FRANK: I'm a massage therapist.

JAMIE: Cool. Very cool.

FRANK: Congratulations on being a famous journalist.

JAMIE: I'm—whoa, I'm not a famous journalist.

FRANK: Well you're all over the internet, you were very easy to find.

JAMIE: . . . thank you?

(They share an uneasy laugh.)

FRANK: You did a, a Fulbright, right?

JAMIE: Oh God, almost ten years ago.

FRANK: Well I don't even really know what that is, but I know it's awesome.

JAMIE: Thanks. It's—it was cool, yeah dude, thanks.

FRANK: And you—I don't see a ring, / but—

JAMIE: Not married, no. Haven't done that yet.

FRANK: But I'm sure you have a girlfriend.

JAMIE: I do. Yes.
Paige.

FRANK: Paige. I like that name.

JAMIE: Me too.

FRANK: She's a journalist too?

JAMIE: She, no, she used to be a dancer but she got injured so she had to retire early. Now she's a licensed nutritionist and she's getting her MSW so she can better address the whole / mind-body . . .

FRANK: Oh, that's great, that's exactly the kind of thing I'm into.

JAMIE: Right, I'm sure, massage, that's / like—

FRANK: I'd love to talk to her.

JAMIE: Yeah. Yeah.

(Brief pause.)

FRANK: And you look exactly like—you know those, for missing kids, they use that, like, age advancing technology?

JAMIE: Uh-huh.

FRANK: That's what I thought when I saw your picture online, I was like, that's exactly what Jamie *would* look like.

(Brief pause.)

Because the last time we saw each other we were, I think, seven.

Sorry, maybe a weird thing to say.

JAMIE: No, no. It's just, you look very different.

(An awkward pause.)

FRANK: So I mentioned in my email that I needed to tell you something.

JAMIE: Yeah.

FRANK: I'm sorry to be so mysterious about it, but it's the kind of thing I thought you should hear in person.

JAMIE: Okay.

FRANK: I also thought you might have an idea what it is.

JAMIE: Um. No.

FRANK: Really?

JAMIE: I haven't seen you in twenty-five years. I have no idea.

FRANK: Okay. I believe you.

(Frank takes a moment.)

Sorry, this is my first one of these meetings, I haven't figured out how to do this yet.

(Jamie waits, more and more ill at ease. Frank seems to be on the verge of tears.)

JAMIE: Take your time, dude.

FRANK: Yeah. Thanks.

Arright. Rip off the bandaid, right?

I'm in the process of opening a criminal case. Against my father.

(Long pause. Jamie sits back.)

For sexual / abuse.

JAMIE: Oh, man.

FRANK: So.

JAMIE: Oh, Frank. I'm so sorry, man. Did you just remember, or—?

FRANK: Yes. Um, well—it's complicated.

JAMIE: Sure.

FRANK: There were things that I remembered that I chose not to think about, and there were things I didn't remember until recently, and then there are the things that he's recently described to me that I still don't remember. Yet.

JAMIE: He's cooperating, then?

FRANK: That's not exactly the word I would use, but he's copping to it, yeah.

JAMIE: How's your mom?

FRANK: Uhhhhh, not so good. She's divorcing him. After thirty-six years.

JAMIE: She had no idea.

FRANK: Well. That's complicated too.

(Silence.)

So this is the hard part.

JAMIE: Oh.

(Brief pause.)

Oh.

FRANK: We had a meeting, a few months ago, mediated by a—my parents' minister. And I asked my father if he had ever hurt any of my / friends.
JAMIE: Uh-huh. Wow. Wow.

(Pause.)

FRANK: Which is why I thought you might have some idea what I / wanted to talk to you about.
JAMIE: No, I—no, I gotta be honest, this doesn't really ring a . . . I mean.

(He takes a moment to try to remember.)

I'll think more about it, but my first response? Not . . . um, familiar.

(Silence.)

FRANK: I guess just the one thing I would like to say? Is that if you do remember anything, and you would be willing to talk to the detectives? That could really help. Because I want to make sure he can't hurt anyone else, you know? He taught Sunday school for ten years, Jamie. When I was older, and not as . . . whatever, not as interesting to him anymore. So I just want to make sure he can't take off and start a new life somewhere else and touch another little kid. You know?
JAMIE: I understand, man, and I think what you're doing is great, and really brave, but I don't remember anything. Sorry. Maybe one of the other, uh—meetings you have, you'll have more luck.
FRANK: Well . . . based on what he described, I thought you would be the most likely one to remember. That's all.

(Brief pause.)

JAMIE: Yeah, sorry, no.
     I'm so sorry that happened to you, man.

(Pause.)

FRANK: Thanks.

(Jamie checks his phone.)

     If you have to go—
JAMIE: Yeah, shit, I'm, I'm a little late for a meeting.

(He picks up the check from the table.)

FRANK: I apologize if I did this—if it was clumsy, or I made you
     / uncomfortable—
JAMIE: No, no, dude, don't worry about it.
FRANK *(Emotionally)*: I'm really happy to see you, Jamie. I know
     you don't feel the same way about me, but. I just want
     you to know that, that I'm sorry we had to meet like this,
     because those years meant a lot to me and I still really care
     about you.
JAMIE: Thank you.

(Jamie puts some bills on the check.)

FRANK: Sorry.
JAMIE: Not a problem.

*(He stands and extends his hand. Frank stands awkwardly and
shakes.)*

FRANK: You have all my info. In case you do want to get in touch.

JAMIE: Yup! Yup. Good luck, man.
FRANK: Bye, Jamie.

(Jamie begins to exit.)

Jamie.

(Jamie stops, looking transparently hassled, and turns.)

JAMIE: What, dude?
FRANK: I know you know this, but. It's nothing to be ashamed of.

(Jamie exits.)

Scene Two

Jamie gets home. Paige is watching TV and eating Pirate's Booty. She looks up when he comes in, then looks miserably back at the TV. She continues to eat. Jamie stands, looking at her for a long moment.

JAMIE: Paige.

(She looks at him. He doesn't speak. She looks back at the TV.)

I owe you an apology.

(She says nothing.)

I'm sorry. I freaked out. I wasn't prepared for that and I freaked out and I'm sorry. And I want to start over, with the conversation, I want to forget about last night and start over.

PAIGE: I don't know how we can start over when you've already made your feelings so incredibly clear.

JAMIE: Those weren't my feelings. That was shock.

PAIGE: That was shitty.

JAMIE: Yes.

PAIGE: That was really fucking shitty, Jamie. I thought about going to my sister's, I thought about leaving.

JAMIE: I'm glad you didn't.

PAIGE: Well I thought one of us had to behave like an actual adult.

JAMIE: I'm glad you're here. I was scared you wouldn't be here. I'm so happy to see you.

(Pause. She turns off the TV.)

PAIGE: Okay, talk.

JAMIE: Well. First of all. I want you to know that I don't blame you, for anything. I know it may have seemed / like I did—

PAIGE: Yeah, it did seem that way, especially when you kept saying, "What the fuck happened?" over and over again, as though it's totally my responsibility, as though you think I might have done it on purpose.

JAMIE: So I'm apologizing for that.

PAIGE: Do you?

JAMIE: What?

PAIGE: Think I did it on purpose?

JAMIE: No. I don't.

(Brief pause.)

PAIGE: Okay. Go on.

JAMIE: And second, I want to say that I consider this an open conversation. I want to hear what you want. That's what I didn't do last night, I didn't / ask you what you want.

PAIGE: No. You didn't.

JAMIE: Which should have been my first question.

PAIGE: Yes, it should have been.

JAMIE: So I'm asking you now.

(Pause.)

PAIGE: I want to have it. I mean, of course I want to have it.

JAMIE: Okay. Why?

PAIGE: *Why?*

JAMIE: Please don't snap at me, Paige, I just, I want to hear your reasons.

PAIGE: Because—because I love you, and I don't know what we're waiting for, that's probably the main reason. Because I'm thirty-four and I don't take it for granted that I'm going to have a lot more chances. Because I think we'd be great fucking parents. But I just feel humiliated saying these things to you, because I know you're not sure of me the way I'm sure of you and you don't want to commit to this, so I think that's that.

JAMIE: No, that's not that, I'm listening to you, I'm hearing what you're saying.

PAIGE: I know, baby, that's what you do, you always listen to me. You listen. You don't act.

JAMIE: I need a little time.

Come on, that's not unreasonable, it's a huge decision.

PAIGE: It's not fair for me to carry this thing around not knowing.

JAMIE: Just a—a week? I think—

(He breathes) I think you're probably right, I mean, I think we should probably . . . what am I afraid of, right?

(She looks at him, almost daring to be hopeful.)

Just a week. Okay?

PAIGE: Okay.
JAMIE: Okay.

(He goes to her and kisses her. She holds his face to hers, breathing. A beat.)

How was work?
PAIGE: I skipped class and canceled both my appointments. I didn't feel like I had any business counseling anybody today.
JAMIE: So what did you do?
PAIGE: I sat here and pitied myself, what do you think?
JAMIE: Did you at least call your sister?
PAIGE: No. I can't, I don't know, be witnessed right now.
JAMIE: But—
PAIGE: Baby, you're in no position to scold me about not talking about my feelings, okay?

(Slight pause.)

JAMIE: Fair.
PAIGE: It was really hard, giving you the silent treatment all day, because I was dying to find out what your friend had to tell you.
JAMIE: Who?
PAIGE: Your childhood friend. Frank.
JAMIE: Oh. It was pretty heavy, actually.
PAIGE: Really?
JAMIE: It turns out his father molested him.
PAIGE: Oh God.
JAMIE: Yeah. Apparently he's just figuring it out.
PAIGE: Do you remember him?
JAMIE: His father? No . . . um, I can't picture him. I think he was tall.

PAIGE: Probably all grown-ups seemed tall.

JAMIE: Yeah. I think he was tall, though. And skinny. With glasses. Kind of nervous, like, hover-y.

PAIGE: He definitely sounds like a child molester.

JAMIE: Yeah, maybe I don't actually remember him, maybe I'm just inserting . . .

PAIGE: So he just wanted to make contact with old friends?

JAMIE: I guess so. It was awkward. He's—I remember him being a really needy kid, he kinda used to follow me around, and he's still like that. Only bigger. And gay. Very gay.

PAIGE: Oh baby, you weren't weird, were you? You're always so weird with gay men.

JAMIE: What? No I'm not.

PAIGE: You get all macho. "Man" this, "dude" that. "Man, it's really good to see you, dude."

JAMIE: No I don't.

PAIGE: I bet you anything you did.

JAMIE: I didn't.

PAIGE: I hope you were nice to him.

JAMIE: I was. I just—wasn't really sure what he wanted from me.

PAIGE: Probably just to talk. It's a big deal, to find out you've been sexually abused, it really fucks people up.

JAMIE: But he's an adult, I mean, he's lived a whole life since then.

PAIGE: Maybe.

JAMIE: What do you mean, maybe?

PAIGE: I mean, maybe he's never really gotten that far from it. Like I think when that kind of thing happens you can get, you know. Stuck.

JAMIE: You mean maybe that's why he's gay?

PAIGE: What? God, you are such a Neanderthal.

JAMIE: Sorry, I'm not exactly educated on this subject.

PAIGE: You can see all kinds of symptoms in sexual abuse victims, uh, fears about intimacy, dysfunction in relation-

ships, *sexual* dysfunction, all of which straight people can
have just as easily as gay people.

JAMIE *(A lame attempt at a joke)*: What are you saying?

PAIGE: What?

JAMIE: Nothing. I was just kidding.

(Pause.)

PAIGE: It's very touching that he reached out to you. I think
you should try to be there for him.

JAMIE: I don't know him!

PAIGE: Obviously he still feels a connection to you.

JAMIE: That's totally ridiculous!

PAIGE: I don't think it is.
      And I think it would be good for you.

JAMIE: I'll think about it.

(Pause.)

PAIGE: Sorry, I've been feeling bad since I said the words "sexual dysfunction," I don't want you to think that was some
passive / aggressive—

JAMIE: I don't have that problem anymore.

PAIGE: No, you've been great. Apparently you've been *too* great.

(She smiles hopefully at him, but he doesn't look back at her.)

A week.

(She takes a breath.)

Scene Three

Jamie's parents' house in New Jersey. Cathy is offstage.

CATHY *(Offstage)*: That's great!

JAMIE: I don't know if it's *great*, it's something.

CATHY *(Offstage)*: Is it health insurance?

(She enters, smiling broadly, with two cups of tea.)

JAMIE: No. Sadly no, no health insurance.

CATHY *(Sympathetically)*: Oh.

JAMIE: Virtually none of these jobs come with health insurance.

CATHY: I know, honey, it's absolutely criminal. This is the kind of tea your father calls "sweepings from the forest floor," but I like it. It has . . . I forget what it has in it, but there are health benefits. Memory, maybe?

JAMIE: Ginkgo biloba?

CATHY: No, I take that in a pill, I don't think they've figured out how to put it in tea yet. Go on, about the job.

JAMIE: That's pretty much it, it's a regular column, and I'll get to contribute to some editorial decisions.

CATHY: So you'll be able to stop copyediting?

JAMIE *(Brief pause)*: Well no, not completely.

CATHY: Oh honey, I'm asking all the wrong questions. Just ignore me, say what you were saying.

JAMIE: That's it, I've told you everything.

CATHY: Well the most important thing is being excited about your colleagues.

JAMIE: They're awesome, I'm in great company.

CATHY: I'm going to look it up online as soon as you go and I'll email you something very intelligent to make up for all my gaffes.

JAMIE: It's fine, don't worry about it.

CATHY: It's just that you're such a talented writer, and so much of what I read—the *New York Times*, for crying out loud—

JAMIE: I know.

CATHY: That piece you wrote about the Sudanese family in Queens, I'm still hearing about it, from friends who say it's just stayed with them. You remember Josie Weltman?

JAMIE: Um . . .

CATHY: She's married to Anton in Dad's department—anyway, she thought it was just incredible and she's a writer herself. I thought it was a shame that it wasn't published somewhere more people would see it.

JAMIE: It's okay, Mom, I'm doing okay.

CATHY: I know. How's Paige?

JAMIE: She's fine.

CATHY: How's Rufus?

(Brief pause.)

JAMIE: What?

CATHY: How's Rufus?

JAMIE: Mom. Rufus died.

CATHY: . . . *What?*

JAMIE: Did I not tell you that?

CATHY: When?

JAMIE: Like . . . six months ago?

CATHY: Six *months* ago?

JAMIE: Are you sure I didn't tell you that?

CATHY: What happened?

JAMIE: We're not sure, we think he ate poison. It happened pretty fast.

CATHY: Oh Rufus!

JAMIE: How is it possible I didn't tell you that?

CATHY: I don't know, I'm furious at you, frankly.

JAMIE: Sorry.

CATHY: It's not like we haven't talked.

JAMIE: No, I guess you didn't ask / and I—

CATHY: Well am I supposed to ask every time we talk, how is Rufus, is he dead? I trust you to tell me these things.

JAMIE: I'm really sorry, Mom.

CATHY: He was the last of a long line.

JAMIE: I know. He was a good little guy.

CATHY: He was.

(They both remember Rufus.)

So what made you come out here? Not that I'm not delighted, I am. It's only an hour but we never see you.

JAMIE: You guys could come in to the city.

CATHY: We could, but it's loud, and it's dirty, and the traffic, and there are no grandchildren yet to entice us, did I say that out loud?

JAMIE: You can complain about not seeing me, *or* get in the car and drive to Brooklyn, one or the other.

CATHY: I want to come but your / father—

JAMIE: He says it's you.

CATHY: I worry that I'm bothering you, Paige seems . . . I don't know.

JAMIE: No, what?

CATHY: It's a difficult relationship, the in-law, or not-quite-in-law or whatever you—I get the sense that she needs her space.

JAMIE: She just doesn't know you guys very well. You two actually have a lot in common, in terms of your / work—

CATHY: Oh, I won't make the mistake of trying to talk about work with her / again—

JAMIE: That was a misunderstanding.

CATHY: I wasn't trying to be *critical*—

JAMIE: I know that, Mom, but it's hard to start a new career at her age—

CATHY: And I think it's fantastic, and courageous, and I *said* that!

JAMIE: But also the field has changed, you're approaching it from very different—

CATHY: I was trying to be helpful, you think I was condescending?

JAMIE: No—I . . . no. I said it was a misunderstanding. And it was two years ago.

(*Pause.*)

CATHY: Listen, you love her, so that's all. That's all.

When we retire we'll come in to visit you all the time, you won't be able to get rid of us.

Especially if there's a grandchild involved.

Just saying.

(Pause.)

JAMIE: So Frank Lawrence got in touch with me.

(She tries to remember who Frank Lawrence is.)

Mom. You're really freaking me out.

CATHY: Oh Frank *Lawrence.* That strange, intense little boy
    from Polly's house.

JAMIE: He's still pretty intense.

CATHY: Uh-huh. Gay?

JAMIE: . . . you could tell?

CATHY: Oh sure. Oh yes.

JAMIE: He lives in Ithaca. He's a massage therapist.

(She makes air quotes.)

No, Mom, I think he's actually a massage therapist.

CATHY: Well that's nice, that he got in touch.

JAMIE: Yeah.

(Brief pause.)

He's prosecuting his father for sexual abuse.

(Pause.)

CATHY: Huh.

(She sips her tea.)

JAMIE: That's all?

CATHY: That . . . makes sense. He was a very troubled little
    boy. And his father was so much more attractive than his
    mother, that was always a puzzle. She had that problem

with her thyroid, and those huge protruding eyes, do you remember that?

JAMIE: Protruding eyes?

CATHY: They were halfway out of her head, I was always so afraid it would frighten you.

JAMIE: I don't remember that.

CATHY: It frightened *me*. Poor little Frank. I guess that should have occurred to us, that something awful was happening to him.

(Brief pause.)

JAMIE: You seem very calm about this.

CATHY: It's been such a long time since we've been in touch with them, it seems . . . maybe this is terrible, but it's like hearing about characters in a book, they don't seem very real to me anymore.

JAMIE: Well I had coffee with him. He's very real, and he's very fucked up.

CATHY: Of course he is, honey, I'm sorry.

JAMIE: Also he—never mind.

CATHY: No, what?

JAMIE: He thought. He has it in his head that something could have happened to me.

CATHY: To *you*? Why?

JAMIE: I don't know.

CATHY: What gave him that idea?

(Jamie shrugs—"no idea.")

Do you think something could have happened to you?

JAMIE: . . . no.

CATHY: It sounds like a case of misery loves company, that's what it sounds like.

JAMIE: I just thought I should tell you, since I have such a terrible memory. I thought if anything had happened, I would have told you.

CATHY: I certainly hope so.

JAMIE: Okay. So forget it.

CATHY: I don't like that at all, him contacting you out of the blue and getting you all upset.

JAMIE: I'm not all upset. You're all upset.

CATHY: I'm not upset. I'm just not crazy about the way Frank handled it, that's all.

JAMIE: I think he's looking for other witnesses in the case, that's why he approached me.

CATHY: Is he after money?

JAMIE: I don't think so; I think he wants to get his dad on that list, you know / that list?

CATHY: Oh that list is totally unconstitutional, it's medieval, I'm opposed to Megan's Law, I don't think it's the right way to deal with sex offenders.

JAMIE: Well, I kinda doubt Frank is really thinking in the abstract about the politics at this moment.

CATHY: No, it sounds like he just wants revenge.

JAMIE: Mom. You're being so weird about this.

CATHY: How am I being weird?

JAMIE: You're bizarrely unsympathetic. For a social worker. And a mom. And an otherwise extremely empathetic person.

(She thinks about this.)

CATHY: I'm sorry, honey. I guess it's just too awful to think about.

(She smiles warmly at him. He checks his phone.)

JAMIE: I should either dash to make a train right now or get the next one.

CATHY: Oh, get the next one! Doug will be home any minute and he'll be so disappointed if he misses you!

(He relents.)

JAMIE: How's Casey?

CATHY: I wish you two talked more.

JAMIE: Mom.

CATHY: She's great. She's happy, she loves her job. She's a total delight.

JAMIE: She's still with that guy?

CATHY: I think she's always going to be with "that guy." You didn't hear it from me, but you may need some vacation time to go out to Seattle this fall.

JAMIE: That soon?

CATHY: You didn't hear it from me.

(Suddenly quite emotional) Honey, I just want so much for you to be happy.

JAMIE: I am. Mom, I am, okay? Stop worrying.

(Doug enters, a yoga mat slung over his shoulder.)

CATHY *(Covering, wiping away tears)*: Here he is, the man of the hour.

DOUG *(Regarding Jamie)*: Could it be?

JAMIE: Hey Dad.

DOUG: Cathy, I think I'm hallucinating. I think our grown son is in our living room.

CATHY: It's really him.

DOUG: Hey, kid.

(Jamie goes to his father. They hesitate, then decide on shaking hands.)

How about that.

JAMIE: How was yoga?

DOUG: It was good. It kicked my ass, it was really good. I try to get your mother to come with me—

CATHY: She's a tyrant! This teacher, / she's—

DOUG: This is one of the best yoga teachers in central New Jersey, you can look it up on the blogs, / she's terrific—

CATHY: I work hard all day, and then in my recreational time I have to memorize things in another language?

DOUG: You don't have to memorize / the Sanskrit.

CATHY: She gives you dirty looks! She'll say, okay now everybody get into pashimotonanababafasana and then she'll just stand there and look around to see who doesn't know what she's talking about.

(Cathy points to herself and mouths "me.")

DOUG: Gita's a wonderful teacher.

CATHY: And that's the other thing, she's a white woman from Kansas who goes by Gita. I'm sure her real name is Mary Joe.

(Jamie has been enjoying this familiar performance on his behalf.)

DOUG: So what's the occasion?

(Cathy and Jamie look at each other.)

CATHY: Jamie. Got a wonderful new job.

Scene Four

Paige is with a client: Joelle, a thin, anxious woman in her late teens/early twenties.

Paige is reviewing some paperwork while Joelle waits, trying not to appear nervous.

PAIGE: This looks good, Joelle.
JOELLE *(Embarrassed)*: Thank you.
PAIGE: This looks really good.
JOELLE: Thanks.
PAIGE: Any problems?

(Joelle shakes her head. Paige waits patiently, warmly, to see if Joelle changes her mind.)

JOELLE: I felt sort of freaked out on, um, Thursday . . . ?
PAIGE: The burrito.
JOELLE: Yeah.

PAIGE: Yeah, that was a big step for you. I was happy to see that on here.

JOELLE: I had like a minor panic attack.

PAIGE: But you got through it.

JOELLE: Yeah.

PAIGE: Did you enjoy it?

JOELLE: Um . . . maybe at the beginning, and then I just felt . . .

PAIGE: Anxious.

JOELLE: Yeah.

PAIGE: Were you tempted to purge?

JOELLE *(She thinks)*: No.

PAIGE: That's good. Joelle, look at me.

(She does.)

That's really good.

(Joelle smiles.)

And you had a paper due on Friday, right?

JOELLE: Mm-hm.

PAIGE: How did that go?

JOELLE: Pretty good, I think.

PAIGE: If you think it was pretty good I bet it was great.

JOELLE: I don't know, it was hard getting started, but then it kind of . . . flowed. I felt good about it.

PAIGE: I don't think it's a coincidence that during a week you were eating well your concentration was better too.

JOELLE: I was thinking that, actually, that it was probably connected.

PAIGE: Not that I can promise you that life will be easy if you just feed yourself—

JOELLE: No, I know but—

PAIGE: But—

JOELLE: Yeah. I get it. I think.

(Paige smiles. Pause.)

PAIGE: So what else?

JOELLE: Oh. I've been trying the meditation.

PAIGE: Great! And?

JOELLE *(An apology)*: Um . . .

PAIGE: Not going so well.

JOELLE: No.

PAIGE: What happens?

JOELLE: I feel like I'm doing it for like two seconds, and then I'm like—something flies into my head that's just like completely ridiculous.

PAIGE: Like what?

JOELLE: Like . . . it's embarrassing, like . . . oh my God what if I'm naked in the student center . . . or like aaahhhh there's a penis in the chocolate . . . or like . . .

(She crumples in embarrassment.)

PAIGE *(Processing)*: There's a penis in the chocolate.

JOELLE: Oh my God I can't believe I just told you that.

PAIGE: I'm not laughing at you.

JOELLE: I know, because you're so nice, but it's so embarrassing.

PAIGE: It sounds to me like the thoughts that sort of flood you at those moments might have to do with temptation. Chocolate, with your history, obviously. And—well, we haven't really talked about sex in here.

JOELLE *(Mortified)*: Uh-huh.

PAIGE: But we can. It's certainly a big part of being human.

JOELLE: But do you . . . is it normal for you to talk about that with your patients?

PAIGE: It depends on what you want. As one of your assignments for next time, why don't you think about whether you'd like to talk to me about—if your sex life is part of what you'd like to work on.

(Pause.)

JOELLE: Okay.
	Um, or lack thereof.

(She cringes at her own awkwardness.)

PAIGE: And keep trying the meditation.
JOELLE: Okay.

(Paige writes some notes in Joelle's chart.)

	So you were a dancer? Sorry.
PAIGE: What? Yes, I was a dancer.
JOELLE: I googled you.
PAIGE: Oh.
JOELLE: That must have been . . . like you must have had to work so hard, it's so competitive, right?
PAIGE: It was very hard work, really grueling sometimes, but I loved it.
JOELLE: Why did you stop?
PAIGE: I had an injury. But I would have had to stop in a few years anyway, so the way I look at it, I got a head start.
JOELLE: Do you miss it?

(Brief pause.)

PAIGE: Yes.
JOELLE: You still look like a dancer. You're so pretty.

(Paige smiles and hands Joelle back her food journal. An awkward silence.)

PAIGE: Is there something else?

JOELLE: Um. You didn't weigh me.

PAIGE: Oh shit! Excuse me. Sorry, I forgot. You're right.

JOELLE: I can't believe I reminded you, I like, *dread* it all week.

PAIGE: It's good you did.

(Joelle is removing shoes, belt, jewelry—she is used to this routine. Paige zeroes the scale.)

Okay?

(Joelle takes a deep breath.)

JOELLE: Okay.

(She steps on the scale. They both look.)

PAIGE: Okay.

Scene Five

Jamie and Doug stand in Paige and Jamie's apartment. A short, awkward beat.

DOUG: It's a pretty block, I forgot how pretty it is.

JAMIE: We like it. It's a good time of year for this neighborhood.

DOUG: Will you two get away together at all this summer?

JAMIE: Maybe a weekend trip to Ohio, see Paige's folks. You know, money's tight.

DOUG: Well we could help you out, we'd love to help you out.

JAMIE: You know how I feel about that.

DOUG: But just—an early birthday present, a week somewhere in New England.

JAMIE: Thanks, Dad, no.

Do you want anything, there's coffee—?

DOUG: I'm interrupting the creative process, aren't I?

JAMIE: Don't worry about it, I was kinda blocked.

DOUG: Starting something new?

JAMIE: I did a couple interviews with this aid worker who lost an eye and a few fingers to a roadside bomb in Afghanistan. She's a former academic, a semiotician, so I thought she'd have some / interesting—

DOUG: Well that / sounds . . .

JAMIE: You'd think so right? But I haven't found the . . . I mean, I don't want it just to be a piece about mutilation, I don't want to take advantage / of—

DOUG: Sure, sure.

JAMIE: So. Might have to let this one go.

DOUG: Your mom and I looked up the magazine online, we just loved a few of the things we read. I mean, we think they're very lucky to have *you*, we think you'll bring them to a new level, but they have some good writers.

JAMIE: Mom wrote me a very sweet email about it.

DOUG: We just—she and I agree that this health insurance thing is a complete scandal. When she retires I think your mom is going to get involved in volunteering for single-payer reform, she's really pretty exercised about it.

JAMIE: When are you guys gonna retire? You talk about it / a lot—

DOUG: Oh who knows, we're both workaholics, probably never.

(They smile at each other.)

JAMIE: Do you want to sit down?

DOUG: Do you have a minute?

JAMIE: You drove all the way here, yeah, I have a minute.

(They sit.)

DOUG: Is Paige—?

JAMIE: At work.

DOUG: On a Sunday?

JAMIE: She's trying to keep up the practice she'd been building. And on top of school, it's a lot.

DOUG: And is she almost done with her degree, or . . . ?

JAMIE: Not quite, because she had to finish her bachelor's first, and now she's doing the master's part time. And then there's another few years of supervised / training.

DOUG: Uh-huh, I / see.

JAMIE: It's frustrating, because she's so good at her work, she's so intuitive and compassionate, she just wants to concentrate on her practice, so to spend all this time and money to get a piece of / paper.

DOUG: She'll be glad to have it, though, when all is said and done.

JAMIE *(Not aggressively)*: Maybe. Not everyone feels about formal education the way you and Mom do.

DOUG: Oh I just meant—from a practical standpoint, finding patients, / and—

JAMIE: Sure, that's true.

DOUG: I didn't mean—

JAMIE: No, you're right, it'll help. It's tough, starting your own business.

DOUG: Sure. You two did not take the easy path. I admire that a lot.

(Brief pause.)

JAMIE: So what's up?

DOUG: Uh, Jamie . . . your mom told me about Dennis.

(Brief pause.)

JAMIE: About . . . ?

DOUG: Dennis Lawrence. Frankie's dad.

JAMIE: Was his name Dennis?

DOUG: Yes.

JAMIE: God, that . . . doesn't ring a bell. At all.

DOUG: I was very upset, when she told me that. I'm still upset. She said it, sort of, "oh by the way," the next morning, and . . . I don't understand her attitude about it, I really don't.

JAMIE: I was surprised, I gotta say, I kind of thought she'd flip out, and she seemed like—I don't know, like she already *knew* / or—

DOUG: She didn't know. She did not know, I can tell you that. I think what's happening, she's having some kind of defensive reaction.

JAMIE: Just because it's upsetting?

DOUG: Uh . . . well . . .

This is what I wanted to talk to you about.

(Pause.)

Do you have some memories of being there, as a kid?

JAMIE: Being . . .

DOUG: At the Lawrences'.

JAMIE: Um . . .

No.

DOUG: They had a—I think it was a German shepherd.

(Doug waits. Jamie thinks, then shakes his head.)

And they were way up on the north side, by that abandoned factory building, maybe you remember playing there? With Frank?

JAMIE: Did I go to their house a lot?

DOUG: Uh . . . no, not a lot.

JAMIE: But sometimes?

DOUG: Well, rarely. You used to complain about Frank, you said he followed you around, at Polly's.

JAMIE: Yes, that I remember.

DOUG: So we didn't usually send you over there for play dates, we figured you saw each other enough.

JAMIE: Then . . . ?

DOUG: But there was one, uh. Week. Maybe a week and a half. Not more than two weeks. That you stayed there.

JAMIE: Stayed there, like . . .

DOUG: Yeah. Stayed there.

(Pause.)

JAMIE: Um. Why?

DOUG: Well that gets into a whole story that . . . that really doesn't matter now.

JAMIE: Dad.

DOUG: Your mother and I were having some marital troubles. We've been married almost thirty-four years now and that was the worst part. It wasn't anything—particularly sordid, or—no one was unfaithful—

JAMIE: Whoa, whoa.

DOUG: Your sister was about four months old, and I still can't say this to Cathy but I think the whole thing was basically because of postpartem. They have drugs now that will take care of it but back then you just suffered, and she really, really suffered. And I was—God was I—? I wasn't much older than *you*, think about that, with two little kids, and maybe not yet the, well, the sensitive and understanding man you see before you, and I didn't. Get it. And at some point I basically said you need to cut this out or I'm leaving. Which, for future reference, is not what you say to a clinically depressed woman who has just borne your second child. I was an asshole. I was a real asshole. And she fell apart. And she threatened suicide. And we didn't think it was good for you to be around that so we asked the Lawrences to take you for a little while as we got through the worst of it.

JAMIE: What about Nana and Pop-Pop?

DOUG: What about them?

JAMIE: Why didn't they take me?

DOUG: Oh. Because your mother didn't want to tell them. I guess I didn't either, when I think about it.

JAMIE: What about the—the Levines, or the Rosses, or the Pascarellas—any of your good friends?

DOUG: Same reason.

JAMIE: You were embarrassed.

DOUG: Well . . . it was a different time, people weren't really talking about those things.

JAMIE: It was the early eighties in a college town, Dad, it wasn't Victorian England.

DOUG: I guess we were embarrassed, yes. It seems silly now, but . . .

JAMIE: But you didn't care what the Lawrences thought of you. Because you didn't like them.

DOUG: Well, that's not exactly fair, but they were outside of our social circle, we only knew them because of Polly. It seemed . . . safer.

JAMIE: "Safer."

(Pause.)

DOUG: Oh, Jamie. We don't think anything could have happened to you. We warned you about that kind of thing, you would have told us. You were, even at that age, you had a very adult quality, you were very self-possessed.

JAMIE: How old was I?

DOUG: If Casey was four months, you were . . . almost five.

(Pause.)

JAMIE: Did I see you? During that week?

DOUG: Yes. Maybe not enough. You still went to Polly's during the day, and I know we saw you a few times, separately, but we were pretty . . . preoccupied.

JAMIE: Wasn't I homesick?

DOUG: You didn't complain. The Lawrences . . .

(He trails off, unable to finish.)

JAMIE: What. Dad, what?

DOUG: I remember them saying how "good" you were. When we picked you up. How you had been so "good." I remember feeling very proud. Feeling like you were the most mature and reasonable one out of all of us.

It seemed like the best thing to do at the time.

JAMIE: Sure.

DOUG: You don't remember any of this?

JAMIE: Nope.

DOUG: You don't think . . .

(Pause.)

JAMIE: No. I don't think so.

(Doug exhales, extremely relieved.)

DOUG: I've been living in hell since your mom told me this, kiddo, I didn't sleep at all last night.

JAMIE: Well you can forget about it. Nothing happened. I'm fine.

DOUG: I know. I know you're fine, but shit, I'm glad to hear that.

JAMIE: I mean even if something *had* happened, which it didn't, I'm thirty-two years old, I'm all the things I was three days ago, before I saw Frank. I have a career, and a beautiful girlfriend, I don't buy into this idea that something that may have happened when I was four can change all that, I just, I don't buy it.

DOUG: Right. That's absolutely right.

(Brief pause.)

But you don't think anything did happen.

JAMIE: No. I don't.

DOUG: Good. Good.

(Doug reaches over and gives Jamie's shoulder a squeeze, or a similarly awkward father/son gesture. Pause.)

JAMIE: Dad . . .

DOUG: Yeah?
   What?

(Jamie redirects.)

JAMIE: Thanks for coming by.

DOUG: We wish we saw you more. It's silly that we don't.

(Jamie smiles half-heartedly.)

Scene Six

The nursing home. Polly sits in a wheelchair, gazing off absently.
She wears thick glasses.

Jamie enters. He stops and stands looking at her for a little while.
He approaches gingerly.

JAMIE: Polly.

(She looks at him. Recognition and confusion simultaneously
flood her features.)

POLLY: Hello . . .
JAMIE: It's Jamie. Jamie Perrin.
POLLY: . . . Jamie? I can't believe it!
JAMIE: It's really me.
POLLY: I think I must be dreaming!
JAMIE: Nope.
POLLY: Come here.

(He comes close to her and stoops. She touches his face.)

Look at you. You're so *old*. You have wrinkles here *(She touches between his eyes)* and here. *(She touches his crow's feet)* You were such a tiny thing.

JAMIE: It's not polite to point out a gentleman's wrinkles, Polly.

POLLY: What happened to you?

(He laughs.)

JAMIE: I just grew up, that's all.

POLLY: Jamie Perrin.

JAMIE: Yup. That's me.

(She laughs, delighted.)

POLLY: Well sit down! Tell me everything! Do you have a girl-friend?

JAMIE: Same one I told you about last time. Paige.

POLLY: Paige. How long have you been together?

JAMIE: Almost six years.

POLLY: Oh! So you're married.

JAMIE: Nn—no.

POLLY: Oh.

JAMIE: No, not married.

POLLY: And why is that?

JAMIE: Well . . . lots of reasons, ideologically . . . you know, discrimination against our gay friends, who can't get married, and, uh, it being fundamentally a religious institution, neither of us being religious . . .

(She regards him skeptically.)

And how are *you*?

POLLY: Me? Oh, I'm fine. It's very nice here. The food is good. A lot of people complain, but I think it's pretty good.

JAMIE: Good.

POLLY: And you know Frank came to see me yesterday.

JAMIE: . . . *Really.*

POLLY: Maybe it wasn't yesterday. You remember Frank?

JAMIE: Of course.

POLLY: He was such a funny little kid.

JAMIE: Yeah.

POLLY: I always worried about him. You know he used to write me from prison?

JAMIE: Frank was in prison?

POLLY: Sure, a couple of times.

JAMIE: Do you know . . . um, why?

POLLY: Well it was . . . a few different things. He always had problems. You remember how he used to lie.

JAMIE: . . . No.

POLLY: But he seems all right. He turned out all right, after all that. All the troubles his father had.

JAMIE: You knew about that?

(Polly looks at him.)

POLLY: Well of course I knew, about Dennis being out of work on and off. He used to come around the house and sit with me while I watched you boys, he was bored, that's what I think. It's a terrible thing not to feel useful.

JAMIE: Huh.

POLLY: Frank wanted to tell me . . . what was it he wanted to tell me?

JAMIE: About the signs of spring?

POLLY: Yes! How did you know that? That's exactly it, the signs of spring. He says he still looks out for them. *(She chuckles)*

The things kids remember. Who knows what I said to keep you boys entertained, I was making it up as I went along. Because you know, I never had my own kids.

JAMIE: I know.

POLLY: So what did I know? I was just making it up. The signs of spring. I hardly even remember saying that.

JAMIE: You did great. You were a great babysitter.

POLLY: Well. I did my best.

JAMIE: I didn't know my parents paid you. Did you know that? Until I was in fifth grade, I think, and my mom asked me to bring you a check. I was shocked.

(She laughs.)

POLLY: You thought I took care of you out of the goodness of my heart, is that it?

JAMIE: Well, yeah. I thought you just liked me.

POLLY: I did like you. And I had to finish paying the mortgage, after Rod died. Do you remember Rod?

JAMIE: No.

POLLY: That's a shame.

JAMIE: I think he died before I was born.

POLLY: No . . . did he? It wasn't that long ago . . .

(Thinking about this sends her into some confusion.)

JAMIE: My memory's not as good as Frank's. I don't remember the signs of spring. I wrote down a few things I do remember, about being at your house. Would you like to hear them?

POLLY: Yes, I certainly would.

(Jamie takes out a piece of paper.)

JAMIE: Um.

Sirloin burger soup.

(Polly laughs.)

That's disgusting, looking back.

POLLY: You loved it. Also Chickarina.

JAMIE: Chickarina?

(Jamie laughs and writes this down.)

Hunting for chestnuts, in the fall. And then polishing them with . . . furniture polish?

POLLY: That's right.

JAMIE: And then what did we do with them?

POLLY: You forgot about them, usually, so I threw them out. We also dipped autumn leaves in paraffin wax, do you remember that?

JAMIE: Uh . . .

POLLY: No. You remember the chestnuts but not the leaves, isn't that funny. I thought the leaves were better.

JAMIE: Um.

This is a very faint one . . . being home sick from school, and being at your house, and lying on your sofa, which was . . . I think scratchy.

POLLY: Our sofa? No.

JAMIE: It wasn't scratchy?

POLLY: Not as I recall.

JAMIE: Okay, then I must be thinking of . . .

Oh. Yeah. This is the last one, but it's really clear. You took us to play in that creek, down at the end of Sixth Avenue.

POLLY: "What was he doing, the great god Pan . . ."

JAMIE: What?

POLLY: That's what I used to recite to you, on our way to the creek. "What was he doing, the great god Pan / Down in the reeds by the river? / Spreading ruin and" . . . something, something, I don't remember, isn't that terrible.

JAMIE: I feel like I almost remember that.

POLLY: Look it up. It's by, um . . .

(She can't remember. She is frustrated and embarrassed. He rescues her.)

JAMIE: Well, by the creek, there was that vine.

(Polly chuckles.)

You remember?

(She nods.)

And the older kids would always swing across it but you wouldn't let us. But we must have been whining and whining and you finally decided you would try it out first to see if it was safe.

POLLY *(Laughing)*: Oh, Lord.

JAMIE: Which we thought was pretty cool, Polly swinging on a vine like Tarzan across the creek. You got major points from us on that.

And I still remember . . .

I still remember you taking a few steps back and running, and I don't think I had ever seen you run before, and it looked . . . and then you jumped, and you swung, and the vine broke, and you fell what seemed like a hundred feet into the water.

(Pause. Polly is no longer laughing.)

And I remember the sound of Frank just wailing. And you came stumbling out of the creek, you were covered in mud, and you had lost your glasses. Your face looked so strange without your glasses. And you ran to Frank and lifted him and held him but he wouldn't stop crying, and I couldn't tell with the mud, but it seemed like you might be crying, too, and I stood a little bit away and covered my ears and looked at my feet because I didn't like looking at you.

(He folds up the piece of paper and puts it back in his pocket.)

POLLY: Well. That's not exactly how I remember it. I remember it being pretty funny.

Scene Seven

Paige and Jamie's apartment.

PAIGE: I'm completely at a loss.

JAMIE: You shouldn't have read it.

PAIGE: Well I did, and I'm not sorry.

JAMIE: Then I don't know how to have this conversation. I don't know how to be with someone who doesn't trust me.

PAIGE: That's right. You don't know how to be with me. It's a relief to finally hear you say that.

JAMIE: You're not taking any responsibility for this, for going into my / email—

PAIGE: Because a week has past, and you haven't said anything, and I'm losing it, and I have no . . . access to you. That's it. That's what I haven't been able to articulate. I have no access to you. This proves it more than anything. That you would keep that from me.

JAMIE: You're not exactly being compassionate.

PAIGE: You didn't let me. You denied me the opportunity to be compassionate by freezing me out. You told your *mom.* Who you don't even like.

JAMIE: Of course I like my mom, I love my mom, what kind of thing is that to say?

PAIGE: You're not close to your parents. You pretend to be close, as a family, but you're not.

JAMIE: Okay, I'm glad I've provided you with another opportunity for this old refrain, my family isn't really close, we're cold and distant, whereas *your* / family—

PAIGE: Fuck you.

JAMIE: is so close and chummy and perfect and all our problems as a couple originate from my fucked-up cold family as opposed to your actually equally fucked-up *co-dependent* family.

PAIGE: Are you done?

JAMIE: You read my email, you were probably thinking, what, that I was cheating on you?

PAIGE: The thought occurred to me, yes.

JAMIE: So I'm not. So you figured that out.

PAIGE: Oh congratulations, Jamie, I guess I should be grateful to you for that most basic sign of respect.

If you were cheating on me, it would make sense that you would hide it from me, that would be logical. That you would hide this from me, that you might have been . . . that I just, I can't understand.

JAMIE: I am doing my best! Okay? I am doing my best!

(Brief pause.)

I was going to tell you. The timing is pretty fucked up, with everything we have going on, wouldn't you agree? Can you maybe put yourself in my shoes and imagine why I wouldn't have gotten around to telling you?

(*Pause.*)

PAIGE: So you think something might have happened to you?

(*Pause.*)

JAMIE: I don't know. I guess.
PAIGE: Jamie—

(*She goes toward him, he steps away.*)

What do you remember?

JAMIE: Nothing, I don't remember anything. When he first told me, I was pretty sure it was a mistake, and this guy, you know, he's a mess, and he's served prison time apparently, I don't know whether to . . . but I guess I'm starting to think it might be true.

PAIGE: You mean, that you were abused.

JAMIE: Well, that I was—yeah. I guess, yeah.

PAIGE: Like . . . how? Do you have a sense, or—?

JAMIE: How? You want me to speculate about things I don't remember?

PAIGE: I guess I'm just wondering—how severe, for how long, when—?

JAMIE: I don't know, I don't know, and I don't know.

PAIGE: Please don't talk to me like that.

JAMIE: Apparently I stayed there for about a week when I was about four and a half, so probably whatever it was happened then.

PAIGE: A whole week? Why?

JAMIE: Because my parents' marriage almost fell apart. Which I didn't know until three days ago.

PAIGE: God. Jamie.

Well that makes a lot of sense.

(Pause.)

JAMIE: What?

PAIGE: It just, it makes sense to me. I feel this immediate, I don't know, recognition.

JAMIE: Are you intentionally being a bitch or do you actually think that's helpful?

PAIGE: Everything we've been talking about, your emotional distance from me, your fears about / having kids, your sexual problems, it all falls into place.

JAMIE: It's very convenient for you to be able to blame—I do not have sexual problems!

PAIGE: You had serious sexual problems for almost a year.

JAMIE: The same year that you were fat, did you ever think of that? That maybe it wasn't entirely my problem that I didn't want to fuck you?

(She gasps.)

Oh, I'm sorry, was that out of bounds? Am I being an asshole? You know, I really can't help it, because something terrible happened to me when I was a child. By the way, I'm pretty sure you got knocked up on purpose. Oops, did I say that? Sometimes I say shitty mean things like that because I was *sexually abused.*

PAIGE: You know, I did miss a couple pills, and I would have asked you to use a condom if I thought you'd be able to keep it up.

(He looks like he might hit her. The moment passes.)

JAMIE: I'm not even sure anything happened. You don't get to put my whole life, me, in terms of it, you don't get to do that.

(Pause.)

PAIGE: Listen to me. When I had to stop dancing I was bereft. You know this. Twenty-eight years. I had missed so much to be a dancer; I knew nothing else; I had nothing else. And then it was just. Gone. From me. And now it seems like it's happening again. The last six years of my life, with you, all the work I've done, all I've put into us. I can't keep starting over. I need to feel like I'm building something. Do you understand that?

JAMIE: Yes.

PAIGE: And if I'm not building something with you I need to start building something with someone else.

JAMIE: I understand.

PAIGE: How could you not tell me you were going through this?

JAMIE: I don't know.

(A pause. She gets her bag and leaves.)

Paige.

Scene Eight

In darkness.

CATHY: Honey.

> *(Lights up—we see that Cathy and Jamie are on the phone. It is late at night. He has been drinking. They are both out of their houses. She is speaking loudly.)*

Honey, can you hear me?

JAMIE: Yes, Mom, I can hear you fine. You don't have to talk any louder on a cell phone, you know.

CATHY: What? Hold on.

> *(She adjusts something on the phone. She still speaks loudly.)*

What?

JAMIE *(Loudly)*: Yes! I can hear you!

CATHY: Good. I'm still not used to talking on this thing. Am I waking you up?

JAMIE: No.

CATHY: I'm on a walk. On the north side. I love Highland Park this time of year.

JAMIE: You sound old.

CATHY: What?

JAMIE: Your voice, Mom, you sound so old. You sound like an old lady. When did that happen?

CATHY: Have you been drinking?

JAMIE: Yes.

CATHY: How much?

JAMIE: A lot.

CATHY: Is something wrong?

(He can't answer this ridiculous question.)

Honey, I've been feeling terrible about how I reacted last week. When you told me about Frank. Did you get my email?

JAMIE: Yeah.

CATHY: I've been thinking that I really should have figured it out, what was happening. Because we talked about it all the time, me, and Polly, and your dad—"what on earth is going wrong with that child?" And looking back it was completely obvious. And we sent you there, for a week, we . . .

(Pause. Loudly.)

Jamie, can you still hear me?

JAMIE: Loud and clear.

CATHY: You're so quiet over there, I keep thinking the phone cut out. Oh look, here I am at the creek. It's so filthy.

It used to make me crazy that Polly took you here. But I didn't say anything. I treated her like another parent, you know, I didn't like to just tell her what to do, I thought she should be allowed to have her own ideas. Mostly it worked.

JAMIE: What time is it?

CATHY: Oh I don't know, one, two.

JAMIE: What are you doing out?

CATHY: When I was a little girl I was always like this when the weather changed. On the first really warm night I couldn't sleep. Now I'm approaching Polly's house. Did I tell you an orthodox family moved in there? It must be a huge family, they've built all these additions, it's a / monstrosity.

JAMIE: Oh *this* is what I wanted to ask you! Was her sofa scratchy?

CATHY: What?

JAMIE: Was her sofa scratchy? Polly's?

CATHY: Honey, what are you talking about?

JAMIE: I distinctly remember her having a scratchy sofa and she said / it wasn't scratchy—

CATHY: Yes, it was a cheap old thing, and it was scratchy, but / why in the world—?

JAMIE: Right?! How could she not remember it was scratchy? It was *her sofa*!

CATHY: Jamie, she has dementia, give the poor old woman a break.

JAMIE: But it was *so scratchy*! I mean, I barely remember anything, but I remember *that*.

(*Pause.*)

Mom.
    Mom?

CATHY: I'm just, I'm looking at Polly's house.

JAMIE: Don't cry.

CATHY: I'm not.

JAMIE: Mom.

(Pause.)

CATHY: We don't really say "I love you" in our family. We didn't say it in my household, growing up, but I never imagined when I had my own kids that we wouldn't say it. So many things you expect from yourself that you don't deliver on.

JAMIE: You didn't do anything wrong.

CATHY: I feel disappointed about so many things. I don't want you to feel that way. I don't think Casey feels that way but I'm afraid you do.

JAMIE: You can't protect me from feeling disappointed.

CATHY: I want to.

JAMIE: You can't.

(Pause.)

Where are you now?

CATHY: I'm still in front of Polly's.

Where are you?

JAMIE: I'm at the subway. I should go down. Will you walk home, before Dad wakes up and gets worried?

CATHY: If he wakes up he'll call.

JAMIE: Mom, will you go home?

(Brief pause.)

CATHY: Yeah.

(Pause.)

Jamie?

JAMIE: Mm-hm?

CATHY: Paige's birthday is coming up this week. I put something in the mail . . . if she doesn't like it, there's a gift receipt . . .

JAMIE: I'm sure she'll like it.

CATHY: We'd like to take you two out to dinner but we don't want to intrude . . . why don't you let me know, will you? Will you let me know what you need?

(Pause.)

JAMIE: Yeah.

CATHY *(Emotionally)*: Take care, Jamie.

(She hangs up.)

JAMIE: Mom?

Scene Nine

Paige and Joelle; Paige is holding Joelle's food journal.

PAIGE: So what happened here?
JOELLE: I'm not sure.
PAIGE: Last week was such a good week.
JOELLE: Yeah . . . I don't know.
PAIGE: I think you do know.
JOELLE: Um . . . not really.
PAIGE: No?
JOELLE: Uh-uh.

(*Pause.*)

PAIGE: Did you feel anxious last week? After I weighed you?

(*Brief pause.*)

JOELLE: Um, not that I remember.

PAIGE: No?

JOELLE: I always feel a little anxious, but . . .

(Paige waits.)

I mean, it was a lot. For one week.

PAIGE: It was two pounds. Which was great.

JOELLE: We had talked about one pound a week being the goal.

PAIGE: Uh-huh. So did that make you feel angry at me? That you had gained more than one?

JOELLE: No, I just . . . thought I should adjust what I was eating down, like, a little.

PAIGE: Mm-hm.

(She refers to the food journal.)

So that's why on three different days this week you had carrots dipped in salsa for dinner?

(Pause. Joelle looks away.)

You were doing so well for the last few weeks, Joelle, I was really happy with your progress.

JOELLE: Yeah, but it was just *fast*, and I thought your whole philosophy was that I should be in control, so I decided I want to go a little slower.

PAIGE: I do want you to be in control, but part of being in control means not being in thrall to this disease.

JOELLE: If I gained weight at that rate for three months I would be gigantic.

PAIGE: Honey, no you wouldn't, I think you'd look great.

JOELLE: That is so easy for you to say when you're like perfect and gorgeous!

PAIGE: I don't always feel perfect and / gorgeous.

JOELLE: But you *are*, whereas I—

PAIGE: *Honey*—

JOELLE: Stop calling me that.

PAIGE: Calling you—?

JOELLE: I don't want to talk about sex.

(Brief pause.)

PAIGE: What?

JOELLE: You gave me that as an assignment, and I thought about it, and I don't want to talk about my sex life in here.

PAIGE: Okay, you don't have to.

(Pause.)

I'm getting the feeling that last week's meeting really freaked you out. Sometimes recovery can be / scary.

JOELLE: I don't know why it should be such a big deal that I only want to gain one pound a week, that's what we agreed on in the first place.

PAIGE: It's not an exact science, some weeks are going to be a little more, some a little less.

JOELLE: So this week was a little less.

PAIGE: This week I'm sure you *lost* weight, this week was a big step backward.

JOELLE: Well *sorry*.

PAIGE: Hey, what's going on?
    Huh?

(Pause.)

JOELLE: My parents want me to see someone who takes insurance. I told them I wanted to keep working with you, and

I told them about your . . . approach, and everything? But they said . . . I don't know if I can keep seeing you.

PAIGE: It should be up to you who you see, not your parents; you're an adult.

JOELLE: Right, but . . . well I'll try talking to them again, but I'm just saying . . . I'm not sure if it's gonna work out.

(Brief pause.)

PAIGE: If that's what's really going on, I can give you a recommendation, someone really good who takes insurance. But if what's happening is that you're scared of the progress you're making with me and you're running away—

JOELLE: No, that's not it.

PAIGE: Good. Because you're young, you haven't been doing this for that long, you have a *really* good shot at getting better. You could choose not to live a life in the shadow of this idiotic fucking . . . you could *not* get in the habit of losing things. I just want to make sure you understand that.

(She hands Joelle her journal.)

JOELLE: Do I have to get weighed today?

(Pause.)

PAIGE *(Gently, kindly)*: Yeah. You do.

(Joelle stands and removes shoes, jewelry, etc. Paige zeroes the scale. Joelle steps on. They look.)

JOELLE: Sorry.

(Joelle steps off. She puts her shoes and jewelry back on, not looking at Paige. Paige records Joelle's weight.)

Um. I know I owe you for a couple months.

Depending on whether . . . I'll just mail it to you, if I don't see you.

PAIGE: That's fine.

Let me get you that phone number, of . . .

(She trails off, finding the number and paper, turning her back to Joelle.)

JOELLE: 'kay.

I also think, just with what you've already taught me, I could probably do it on my own.

(Pause. Paige keeps her back to Joelle. Joelle looks over at her anxiously, thinking she might be crying.)

I'm really grateful, I hope you . . . For everything you've—I just. I have to do it in my own time, you know?

(Paige nods. She finishes writing and turns back to Joelle.)

PAIGE: Yeah. I do know.

Scene Ten

Outdoors. A beautiful late spring day. Jamie sits with Frank. A silence.

JAMIE: . . . the other thing I've been wondering, is whether his memory is reliable after all this time either. Who knows what was fantasy, what was reality, whether he mixed up what happened with different kids.

FRANK: That's true.

JAMIE: So I can't take what he says as the absolute truth, either, it's just another piece of the puzzle.

FRANK: Right.

(Brief pause.)

JAMIE: Thanks for coming down here again, man, I know it's a long trip.

FRANK: Just because I came doesn't mean I have to tell you. You can still change your mind.

JAMIE: Thanks.

(Pause.)

How's, um. I forget his name. Your boyfriend.

FRANK: I don't think I told you his name. Lucas. He's good. He's uh . . .

(He smiles, thinking of something.)

Crazy. He's / great.

JAMIE: I also think there's a reason for forgetting. Evolutionarily. This whole pop-psych obsession with uncovering, and uncovering . . . I've been wondering, honestly, if I should be pissed at you for getting in touch.

FRANK: I understand that.

JAMIE: Has anyone else you've contacted, uh . . . remembered anything?

FRANK: No. But I didn't think they would.

JAMIE: Why not?

FRANK: Because they were all, um. According to my dad. Asleep. When / it—

JAMIE: Oh.

FRANK: Because his MO was / to—

JAMIE: Hang on. Not ready yet.

(A silence.)

FRANK: I saw Polly. When I went down to make the official report, in Highland Park.

JAMIE: She told me.

FRANK: You saw her too?

(Jamie nods.)

I didn't recognize her. So weird to think of all the people who mean so much to us and then are just . . . gone. When I moved, losing Polly, and you, I think that was the first time I really experienced grief.

JAMIE: Are you staying in touch with your dad?

FRANK: We haven't had any contact since that meeting, with the minister. I don't plan to speak to him again.

JAMIE: I'm sorry.

FRANK: Me too. It's a fucking shame. I really liked the guy.

(Pause.)

JAMIE: Man, I gotta ask you something, I hope you won't take offense.

FRANK: Okay.

JAMIE: Were you . . . ? In prison?

(Pause.)

FRANK: Huh. Okay.

JAMIE: Sorry, it's just . . .

FRANK: No, I understand. I understand why you'd want to know that. I would have told you, any time you asked, that I was.

JAMIE: Uh-huh.

FRANK: Because I struggled with addiction, for almost nine years, from when I was eighteen / until—

JAMIE: Sorry, you don't have to / explain—

FRANK: No, and I was convicted of two felonies, both non-violent, during that time. Stealing, forging checks.

JAMIE: Okay.

FRANK: I'm not proud of it. But I'm proud of getting better.

(Jamie nods, embarrassed to have asked. A silence.)

How's Paige?

(Jamie weeps. It's a total release. After a moment, Frank reaches over and rubs his back. It's a firm, caring, nonsexual, intimate touch. Jamie gives in to it. After a few moments, he recovers.)

JAMIE: Sorry about that.
FRANK: No problem.
JAMIE: That feels really good.
FRANK: You're like . . . cement, you're a brick back there.
JAMIE: Yeah.
     She's getting an abortion. Today. So.
FRANK: Oh . . .
JAMIE: I wanted to have it. I decided. But she felt that we weren't ready. That it would put too much pressure on our relationship. She doesn't feel sure enough, she said. Of me.

(Brief pause.)

Her sister's there with her, she didn't want me to come.
FRANK: She'll be fine.
JAMIE: She has some, um—she's struggled with depression, and other mental health, like—I'm worried—especially since I know it's not what she really wanted, and I've read some women can have a bad, like a hormonal response—
FRANK: She'll be okay, you'll be there, she'll get through it.

(Brief pause.)

JAMIE: Yeah.

FRANK: For what it's worth, I've been in a lot of support groups, for a lot of different shit? And I've seen couples come back from way worse. I mean . . .

(*He thinks of a few examples, decides not to relate them.*)

Way worse. She could have left and had it on her own, if that's what she wanted. Sounds to me like she chose you.

(*Pause.*)

JAMIE: The other thing is that in the presence of *you*, and a minister, and—was your mother there? What makes us think he would be motivated to tell the / truth?

FRANK: Jamie, you know what? Let's not do this.

JAMIE: No, I want to, / I'm just—

FRANK: We don't have to. You have my number, and my email, or if you need to do it in person I could come back, or you could come to / Ithaca.

JAMIE: No, this is ridiculous, I don't know what the fuck I'm so afraid of. We're talking about something that may or may not have happened twenty-seven years ago. I mean it can't be worse than what's going on in my life right *now*, it can't be worse than that.

(*Jamie tries to gauge Frank's reaction to this, but Frank gives nothing away.*)

FRANK: What if I wrote it down? And handed it to you. Then you could decide when, or—*whether* to read it. In your own time.

JAMIE: You must think I'm such a pussy.

FRANK: Nope.

JAMIE: Won't it take a long time? To write it all out?

(Frank considers.)

FRANK: No. Not really.

(Frank puts out his hand. Jamie gets a notebook and pen from his bag and hands it to him. Frank begins to write. Jamie stands and walks some distance away. Perhaps thirty seconds pass.)

JAMIE *(To himself)*:
>   What was he doing, the great god Pan,
>   Down in the reeds by the river?

(Frank looks up.)

>   Spreading ruin and scattering ban,

JAMIE AND FRANK *(Frank is a beat behind—remembering as he hears it)*:
>   Splashing and paddling with hoofs of a goat,
>   And breaking the golden lilies afloat

JAMIE:
>   With the dragon-fly on the river.

(They look at each other for a few moments, and then Frank continues writing. Jamie waits.)

What I should have said to her is that it's great news that she can get pregnant. She was so worried she wouldn't be able to, because she was sick for a while. So that's really good news. That's what I should have said, in the first place.

(Frank is reading over what he has written. Jamie watches him. He makes one correction. He folds it once, twice, and extends it to Jamie. Jamie takes a step toward him. Lights.)

END OF PLAY

Amy Herzog's plays include *After the Revolution* (Williamstown Theatre Festival, Playwrights Horizons, Lilly Award); *4000 Miles* (Lincoln Center Theater, Pulitzer Prize finalist, Obie Award for the Best New American Play); *The Great God Pan* (Playwrights Horizons) and *Belleville* (Yale Repertory Theatre, New York Theatre Workshop, finalist for the Susan Smith Blackburn Prize). She has received commissions from Yale Repertory Theatre, Steppenwolf Theatre Company and Playwrights Horizons. Amy is a recipient of the Whiting Writers' Award, the Benjamin H. Danks Award from the American Academy of Arts and Letters, the Helen Merrill Award, the Joan and Joseph F. Cullman Award for Extraordinary Creativity and the *New York Times* Outstanding Playwright Award. She is a Usual Suspect at New York Theatre Workshop and an alumna of Youngblood at Ensemble Studio Theatre, Play Group at Ars Nova and the Soho Rep Writer/Director Lab. She has taught playwriting at Bryn Mawr and Yale, and received an MFA from the Yale School of Drama.